TRACE & LEARN - LETTERS

ALPHABET TRACING WORKBOOK
PRACTICE WORKSHEETS

Tons of practice exercises for your child to learn to write the letters of the alphabet and acquire this endlessly rewarding skill in a few weeks with regular practice.

By Shobha

VOLUME I

A	a		N	n	nest
B	b		O	o	
C	c		P	p	
D	d		Q	q	quintet
E	e		R	r	
F	f		S	s	
G	g		T	t	
H	h		U	u	
I	i		V	v	viking
J	j	jaguar	W	w	
K	k		X	x	
L	l		Y	y	yo-yo
M	m		Z	z	

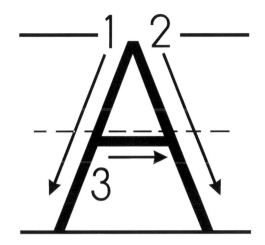

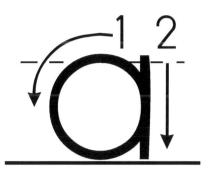

A is for **A**lligator

Have your child trace the letters "A" and "a" on the dotted line. Follow the direction and sequence shown in the example below.

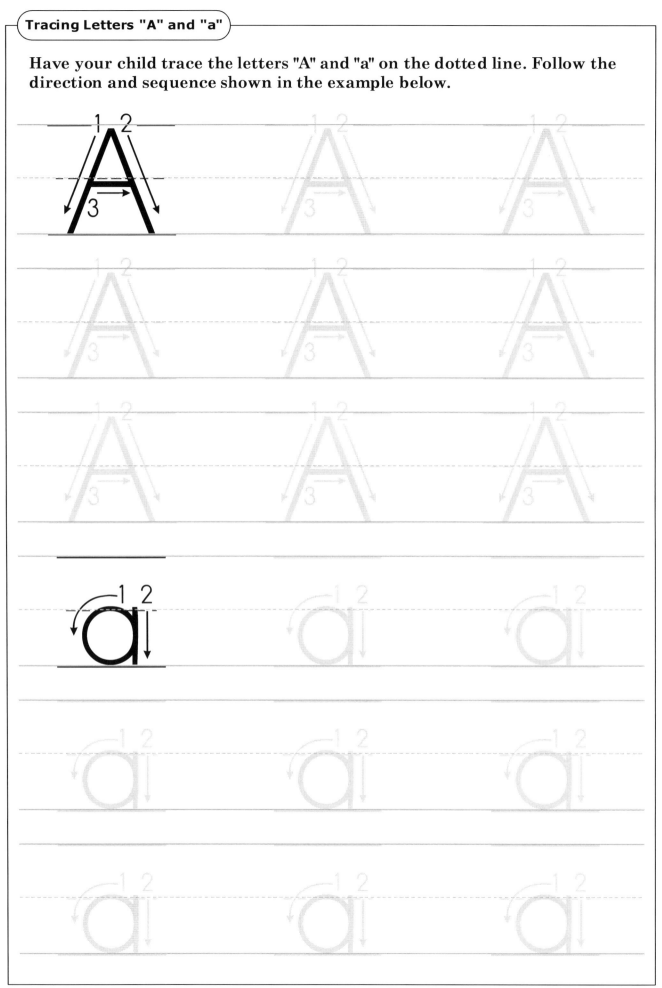

Have your child trace the letters "A" and "a" on the dotted line. Follow the direction and sequence shown in the example below.

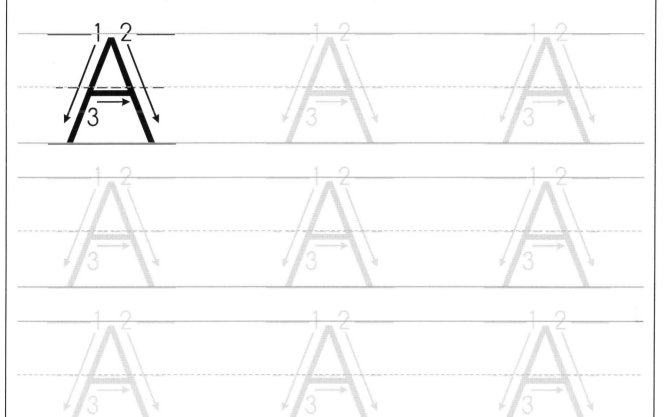

Have your child trace the letters "A" and "a" on the dotted line.

Trace and Learn Letters - Alphabet Tracing Practice Workbook

Have your child trace the letters "A" and "a" on the dotted line.

Have your child trace the letters "A" and "a" on the lines below. Follow the direction and sequence shown in the example. The child should be able to trace letters without the help of dotted lines.

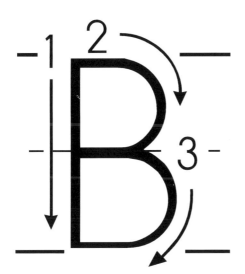

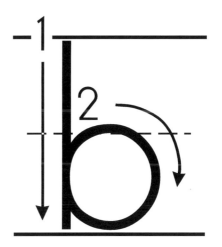

B is for **B**ear

Have your child trace the letters "B" and "b" on the dotted line. Follow the direction and sequence shown in the example below.

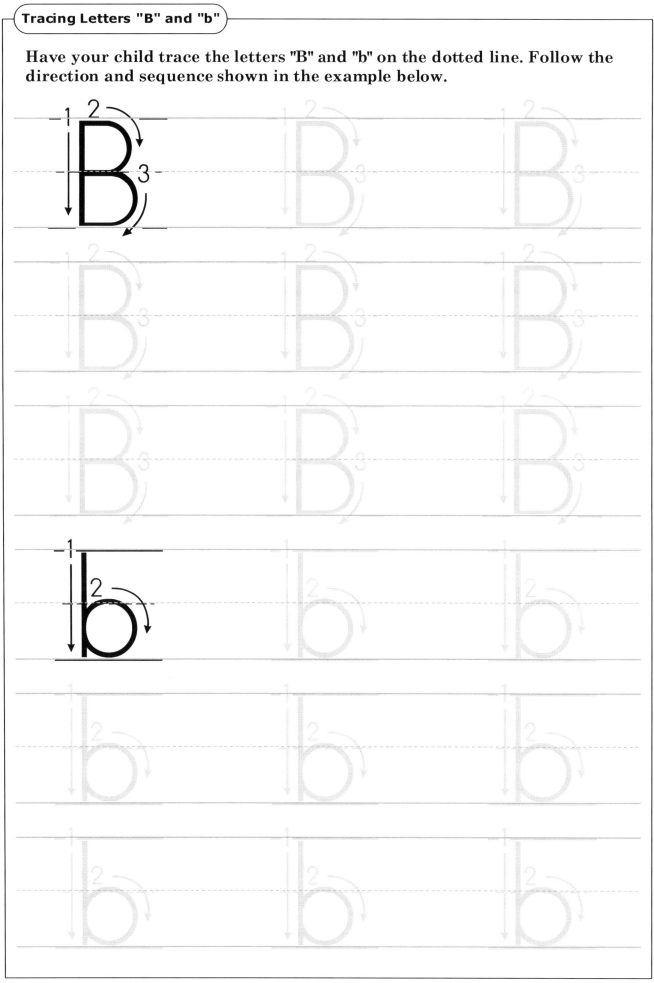

Have your child trace the letters "B" and "b" on the dotted line. Follow the direction and sequence shown in the example below.

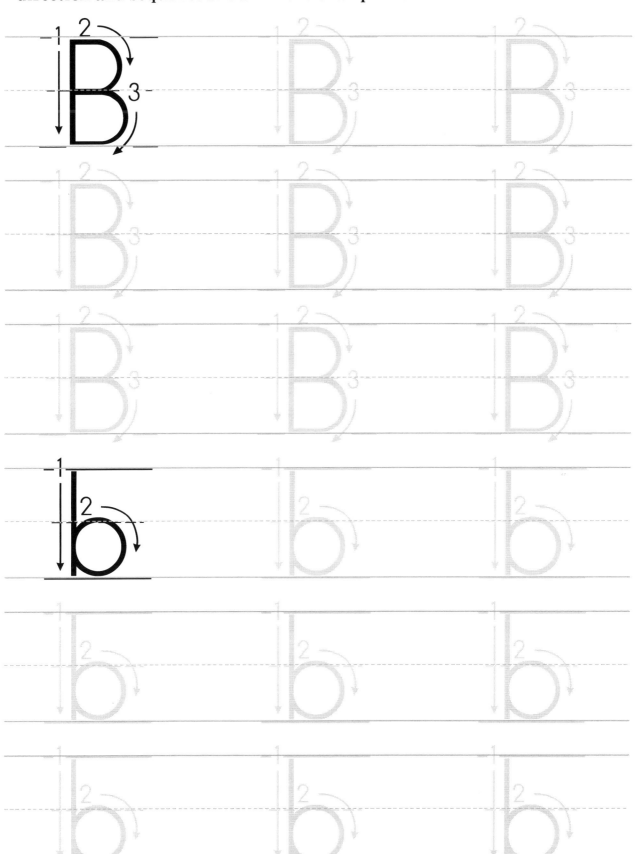

Have your child trace the letters "B" and "b" on the dotted line.

Trace and Learn Letters - Alphabet Tracing Practice Workbook

Have your child trace the letters "B" and "b" on the dotted line.

Have your child trace the letters "B" and "b" on the lines below. Follow the direction and sequence shown in the example. The child should be able to trace letters without the help of dotted lines.

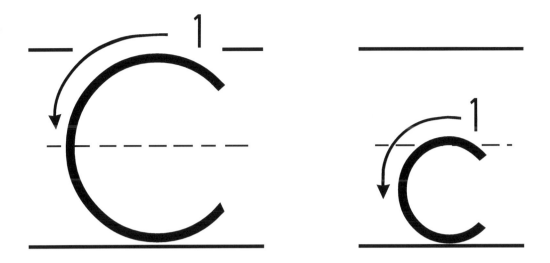

C is for Cat

Have your child trace the letters "C" and "c" on the dotted line. Follow the
direction and sequence shown in the example below.

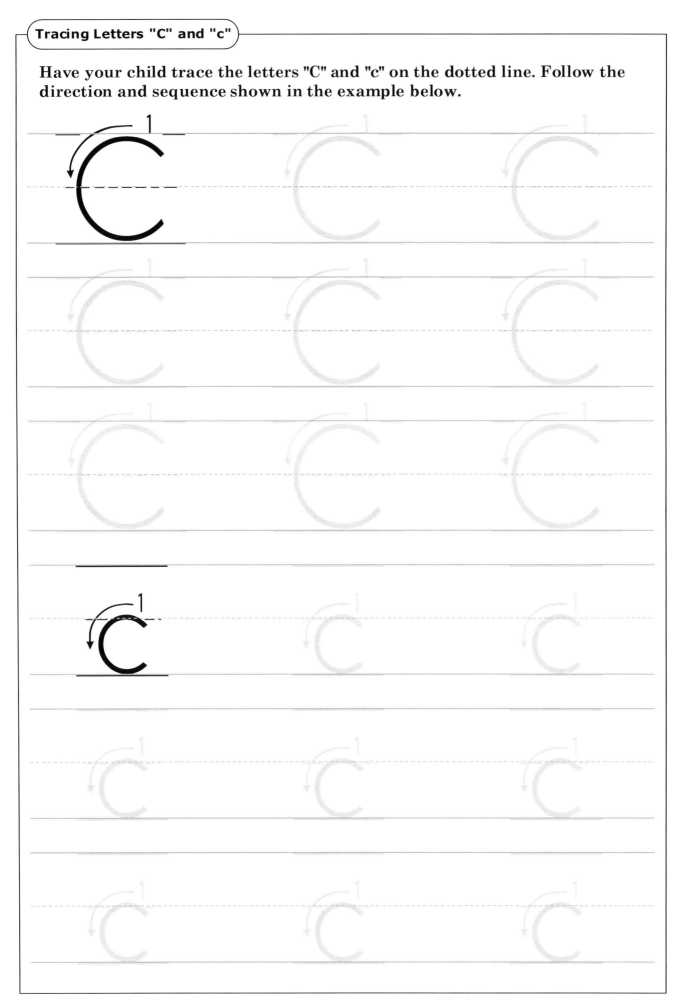

Have your child trace the letters "C" and "c" on the dotted line. Follow the direction and sequence shown in the example below.

Have your child trace the letters "C" and "c" on the dotted line.

Trace and Learn Letters - Alphabet Tracing Practice Workbook

Have your child trace the letters "C" and "c" on the dotted line.

Have your child trace the letters "C" and "c" on the lines below. Follow the direction and sequence shown in the example. The child should be able to trace letters without the help of dotted lines.

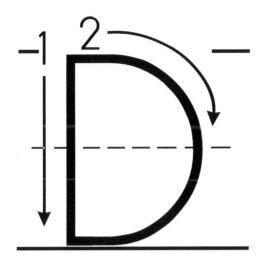
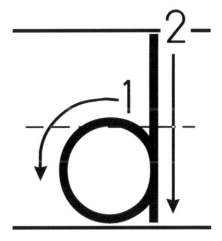

D is for **D**og

Have your child trace the letters "D" and "d" on the dotted line. Follow the direction and sequence shown in the example below.

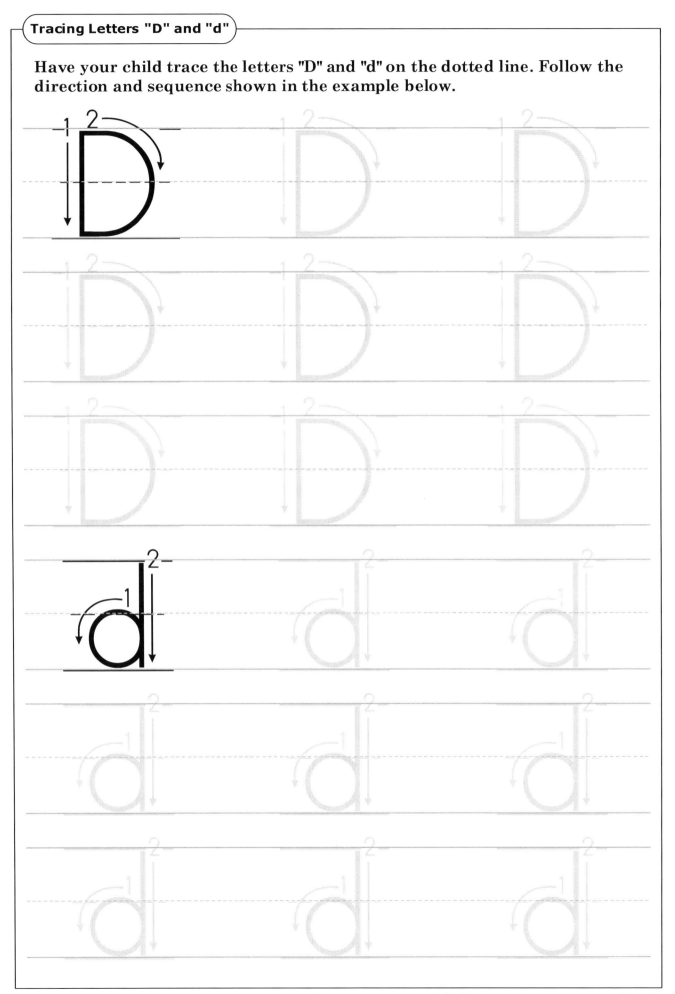

Have your child trace the letters "D" and "d" on the dotted line. Follow the direction and sequence shown in the example below.

Have your child trace the letters "D" and "d" on the dotted line.

Have your child trace the letters "D" and "d" on the dotted line.

Have your child trace the letters "D" and "d" on the lines below. Follow the direction and sequence shown in the example. The child should be able to trace letters without the help of dotted lines.

Trace and Learn Letters - Alphabet Tracing Practice Workbook

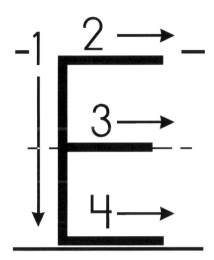

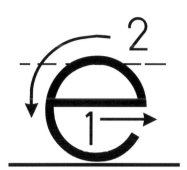

E is for **E**lephant

Have your child trace the letters "E" and "e" on the dotted line. Follow the direction and sequence shown in the example below.

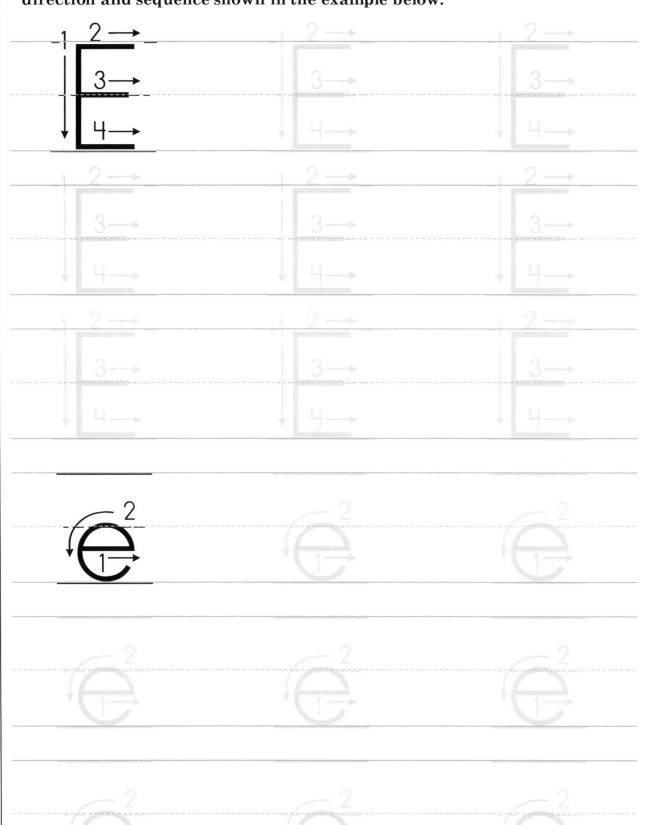

Have your child trace the letters "E" and "e" on the dotted line. Follow the direction and sequence shown in the example below.

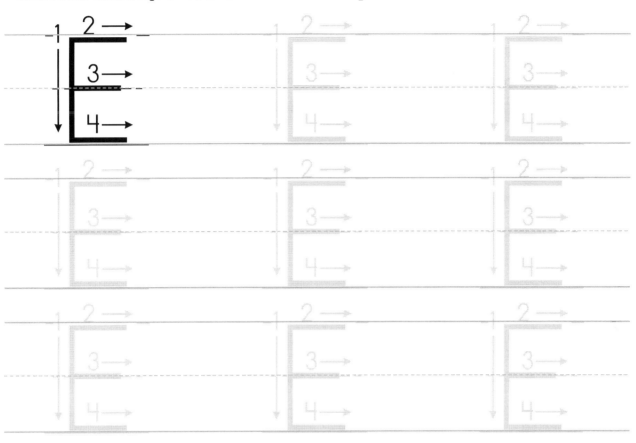

Have your child trace the letters "E" and "e" on the dotted line.

Trace and Learn Letters - Alphabet Tracing Practice Workbook

Have your child trace the letters "E" and "e" on the dotted line.

Have your child trace the letters "E" and "e" on the lines below. Follow the direction and sequence shown in the example. The child should be able to trace letters without the help of dotted lines.

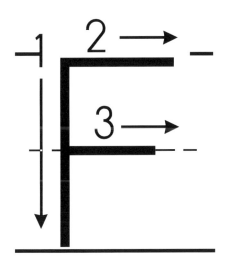
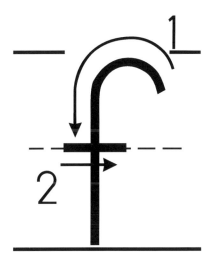

F is for Fox

Have your child trace the letters "F" and "f" on the dotted line. Follow the direction and sequence shown in the example below.

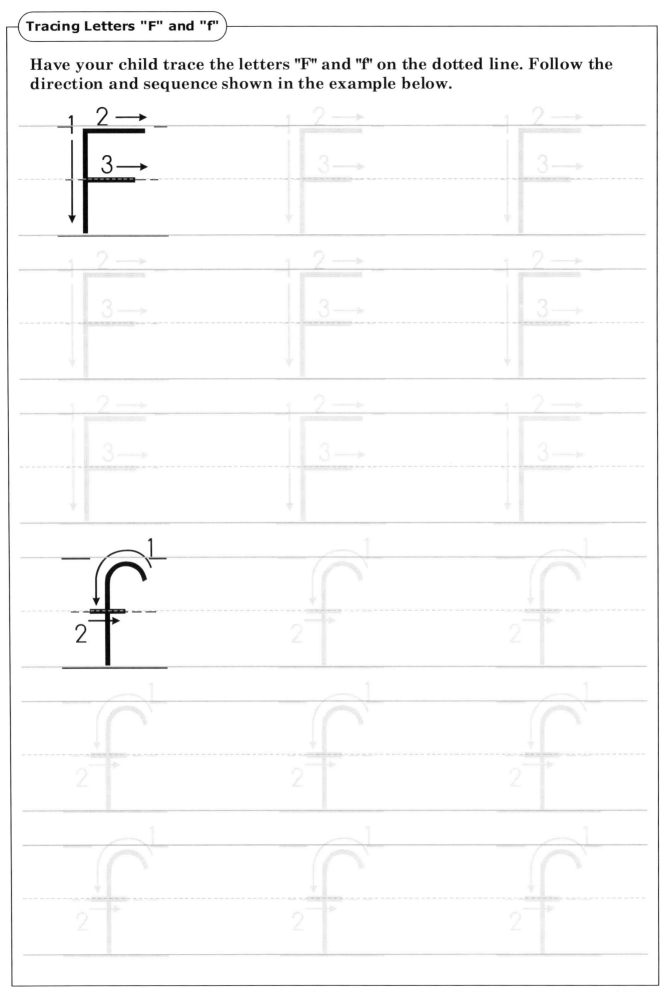

Have your child trace the letters "F" and "f" on the dotted line. Follow the direction and sequence shown in the example below.

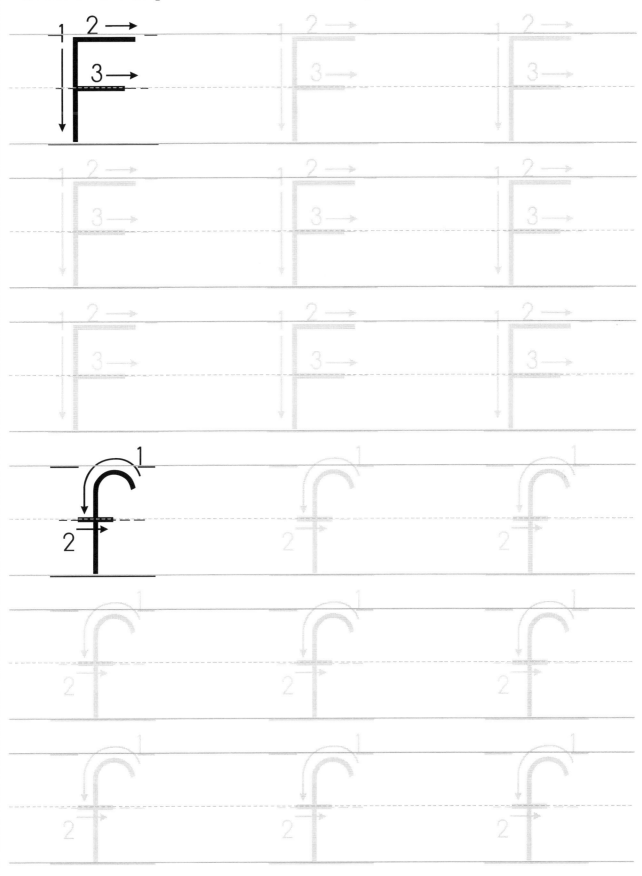

Have your child trace the letters "F" and "f" on the dotted line.

Trace and Learn Letters - Alphabet Tracing Practice Workbook

Have your child trace the letters "F" and "f" on the dotted line.

Have your child trace the letters "F" and "f" on the lines below. Follow the direction and sequence shown in the example. The child should be able to trace letters without the help of dotted lines.

G is for **G**iraffe

Have your child trace the letters "G" and "g" on the dotted line. Follow the direction and sequence shown in the example below.

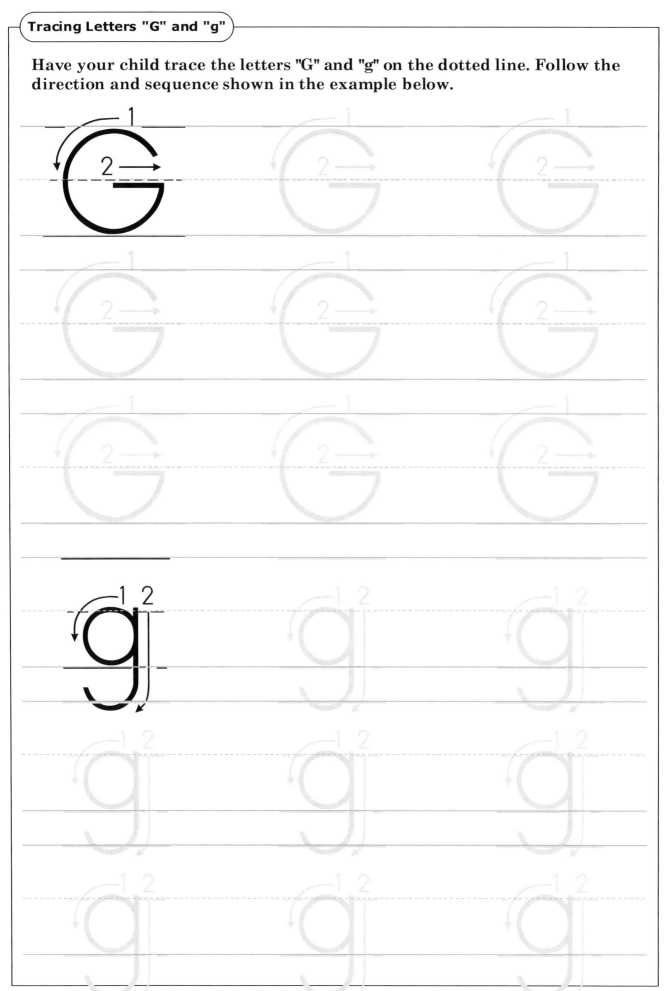

Have your child trace the letters "G" and "g" on the dotted line. Follow the direction and sequence shown in the example below.

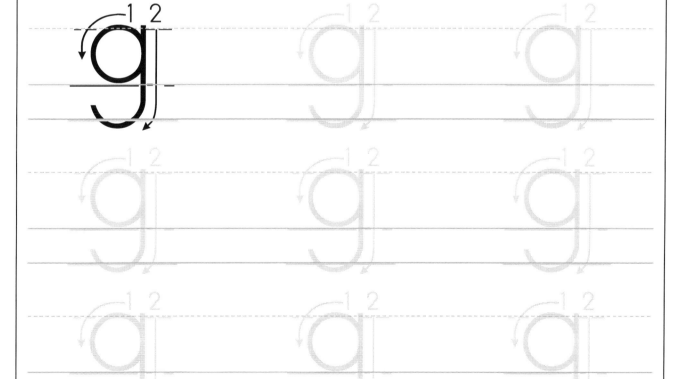

Have your child trace the letters "G" and "g" on the dotted line.

Have your child trace the letters "G" and "g" on the dotted line.

Have your child trace the letters "G" and "g" on the lines below. Follow the direction and sequence shown in the example. The child should be able to trace letters without the help of dotted lines.

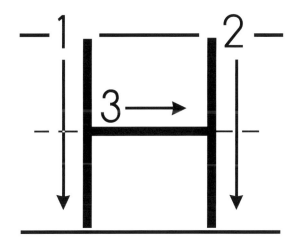
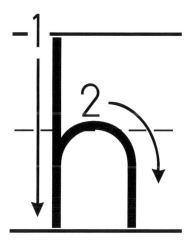

H is for Hare

Have your child trace the letters "H" and "h" on the dotted line. Follow the direction and sequence shown in the example below.

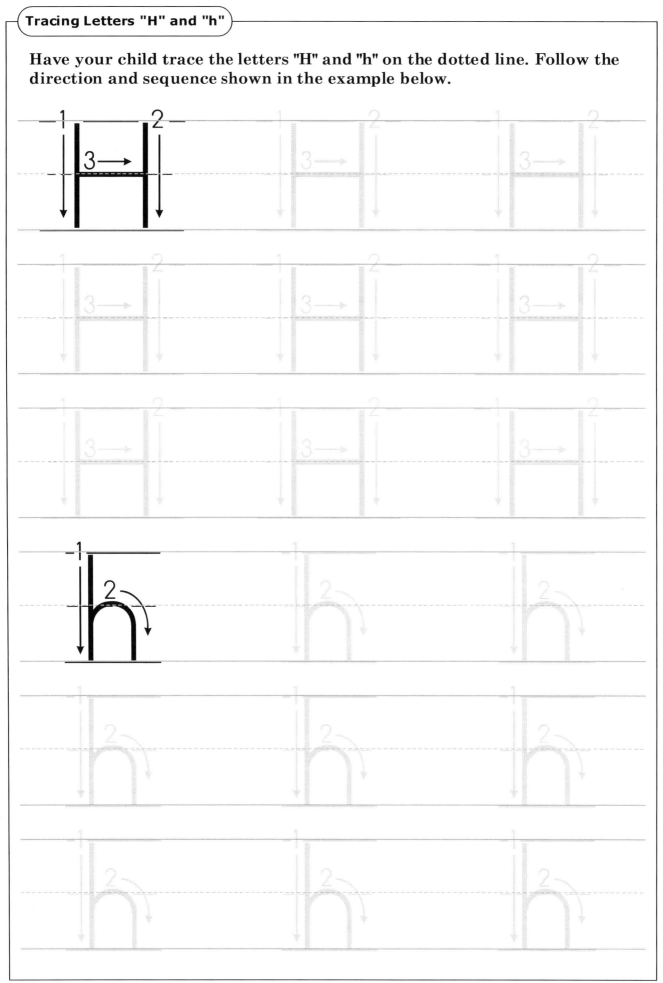

Have your child trace the letters "H" and "h" on the dotted line. Follow the direction and sequence shown in the example below.

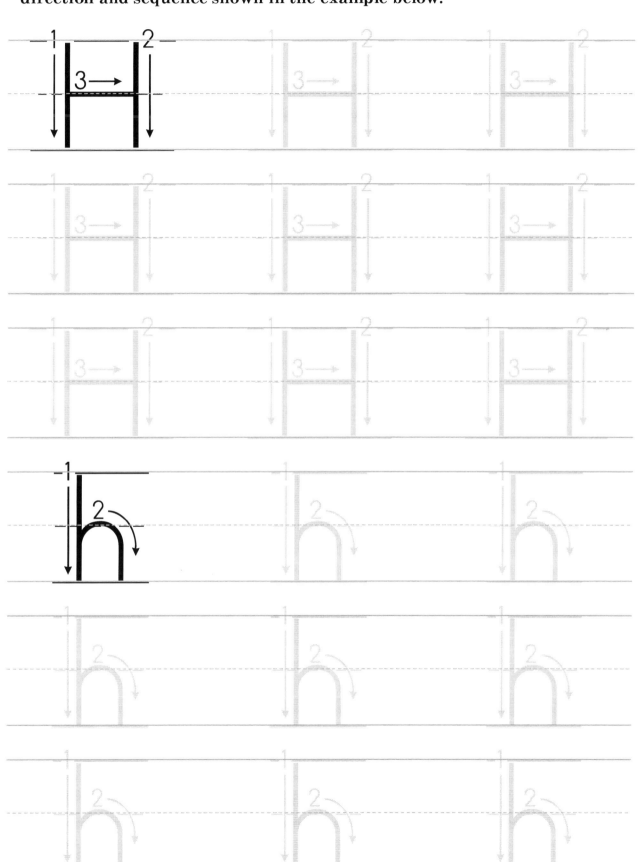

Have your child trace the letters "H" and "h" on the dotted line.

Trace and Learn Letters - Alphabet Tracing Practice Workbook

Have your child trace the letters "H" and "h" on the dotted line.

Have your child trace the letters "H" and "h" on the lines below. Follow the direction and sequence shown in the example. The child should be able to trace letters without the help of dotted lines.

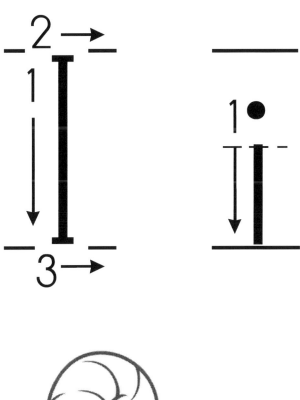

I is for Ibex

Have your child trace the letters "I" and "i" on the dotted line. Follow the direction and sequence shown in the example below.

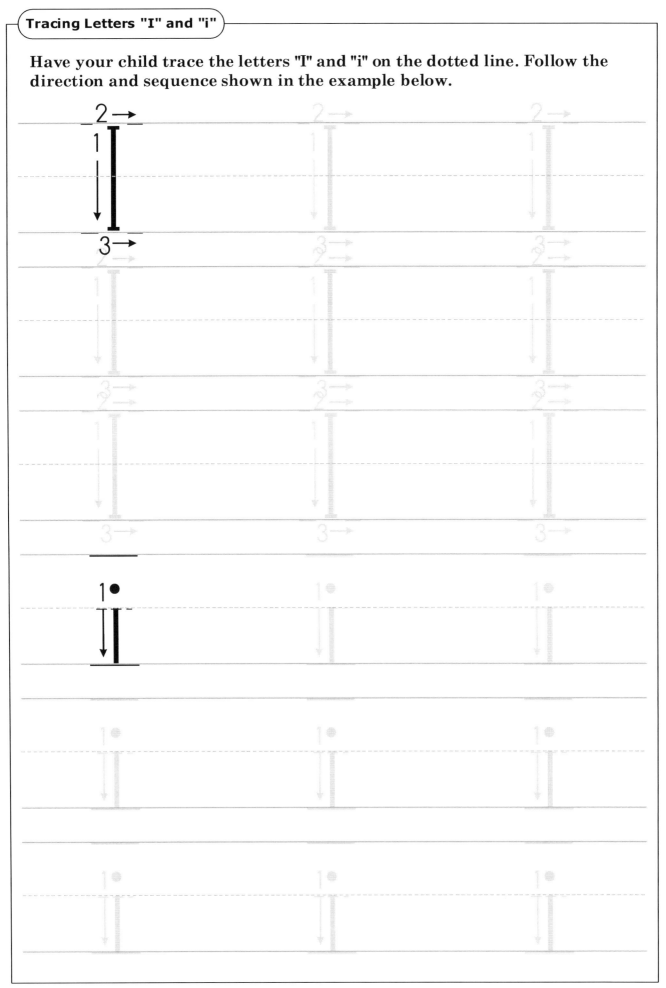

Trace and Learn Letters - Alphabet Tracing Practice Workbook

Have your child trace the letters "I" and "i" on the dotted line. Follow the direction and sequence shown in the example below.

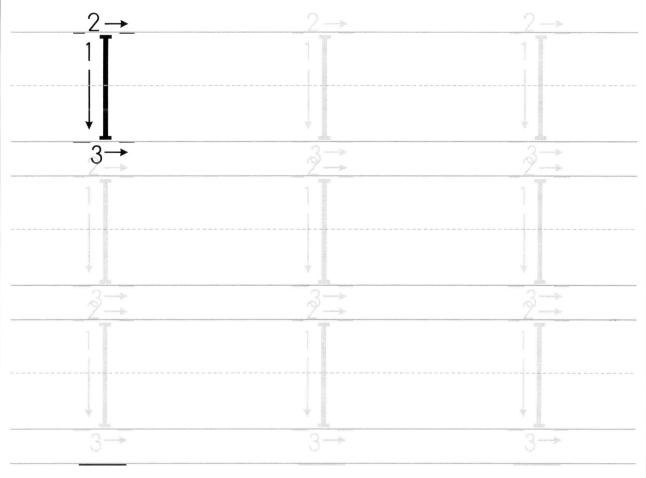

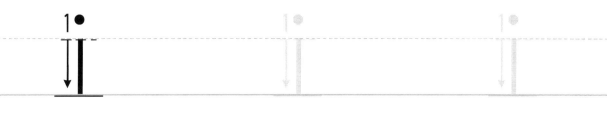

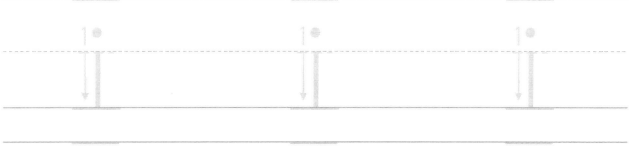

Have your child trace the letters "I" and "i" on the dotted line.

Trace and Learn Letters - Alphabet Tracing Practice Workbook

Have your child trace the letters "I" and "i" on the dotted line.

Have your child trace the letters "I" and "i" on the lines below. Follow the direction and sequence shown in the example. The child should be able to trace letters without the help of dotted lines.

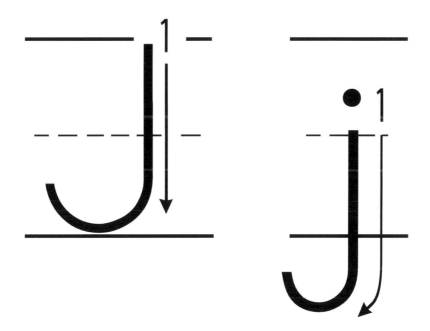

J is for Jaguar

Have your child trace the letters "J" and "j" on the dotted line. Follow the direction and sequence shown in the example below.

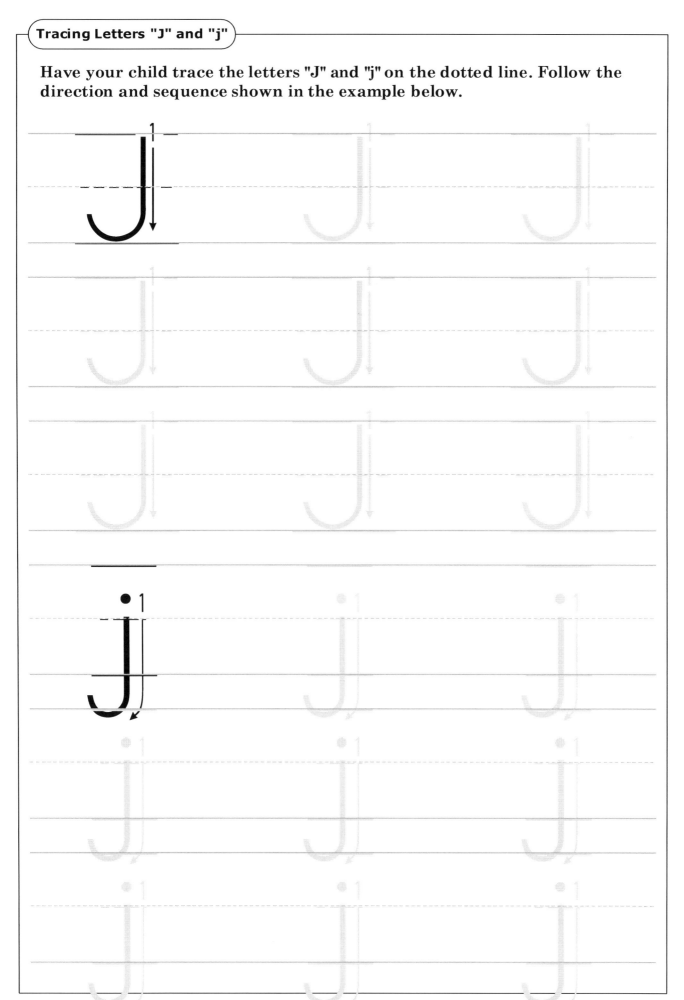

Have your child trace the letters "J" and "j" on the dotted line. Follow the direction and sequence shown in the example below.

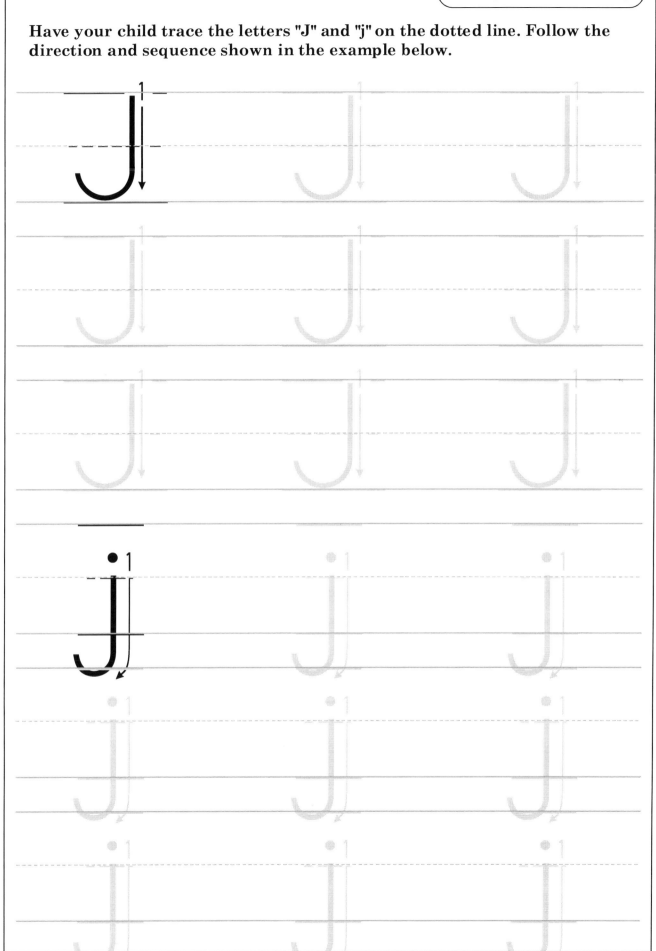

Have your child trace the letters "J" and "j" on the dotted line.

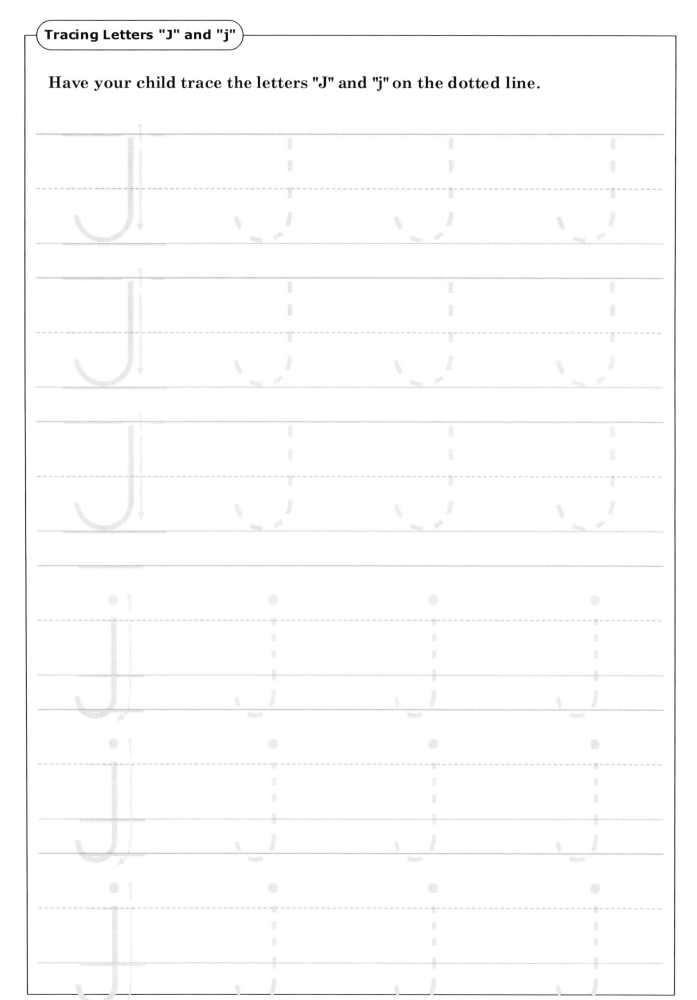

Have your child trace the letters "J" and "j" on the dotted line.

Have your child trace the letters "J" and "j" on the lines below. Follow the direction and sequence shown in the example. The child should be able to trace letters without the help of dotted lines.

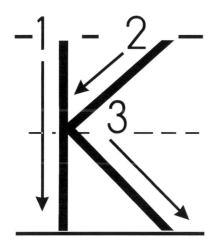 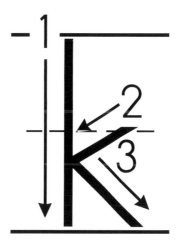

K is for **K**angaroo

Have your child trace the letters "K" and "k" on the dotted line. Follow the direction and sequence shown in the example below.

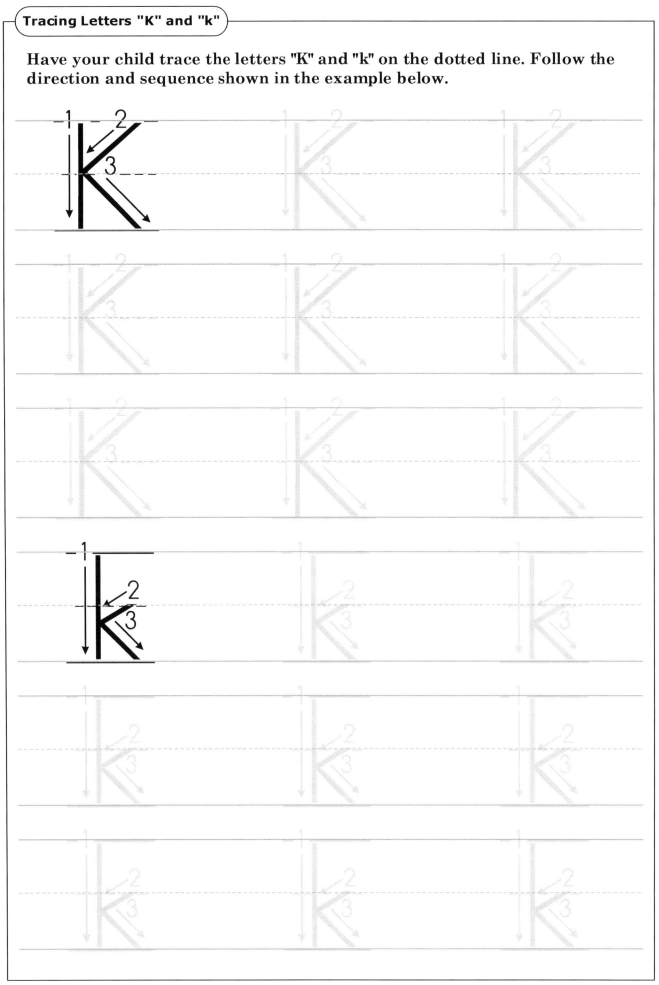

Have your child trace the letters "K" and "k" on the dotted line. Follow the direction and sequence shown in the example below.

Have your child trace the letters "K" and "k" on the dotted line.

Have your child trace the letters "K" and "k" on the dotted line.

Have your child trace the letters "K" and "k" on the lines below. Follow the direction and sequence shown in the example. The child should be able to trace letters without the help of dotted lines.

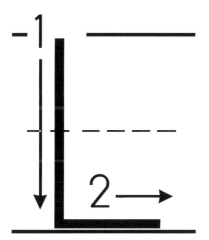
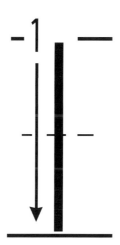

L is for Lion

Have your child trace the letters "L" and "l" on the dotted line. Follow the direction and sequence shown in the example below.

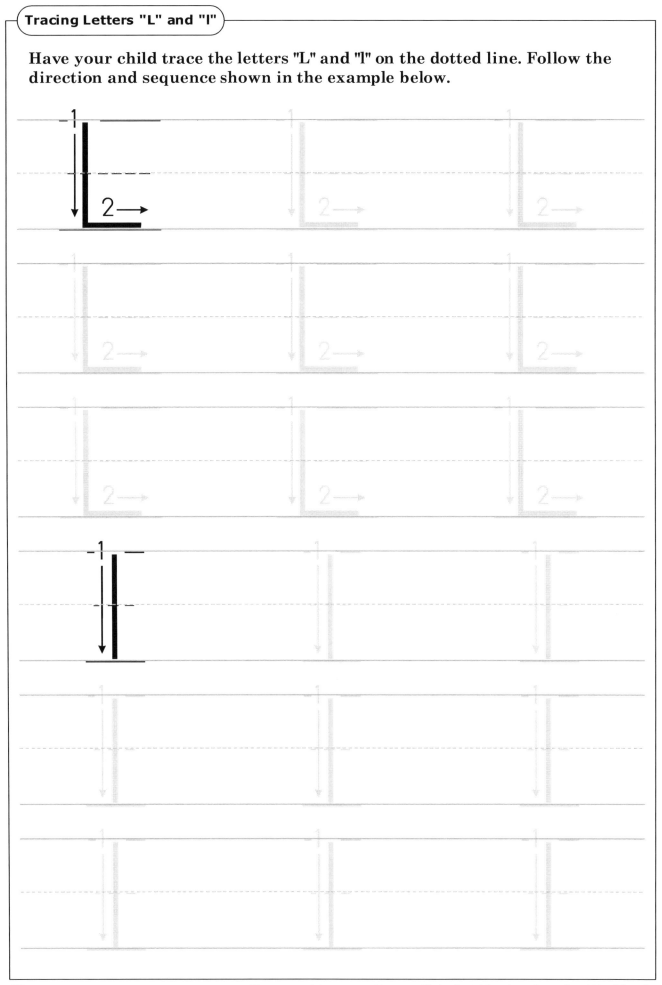

Have your child trace the letters "L" and "l" on the dotted line. Follow the direction and sequence shown in the example below.

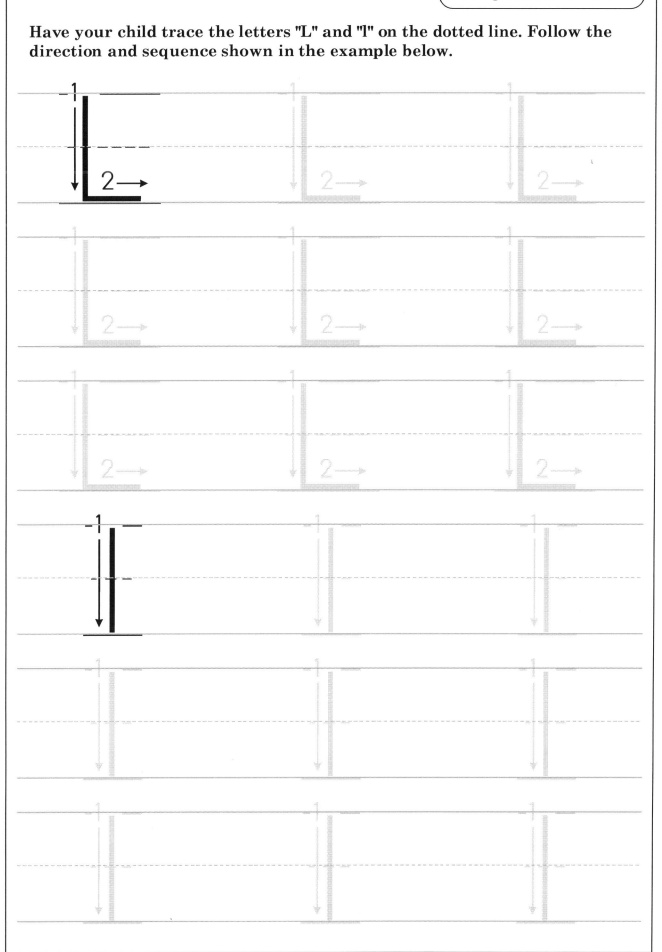

Have your child trace the letters "L" and "l" on the dotted line.

Have your child trace the letters "L" and "l" on the dotted line.

Have your child trace the letters "L" and "l" on the lines below. Follow the direction and sequence shown in the example. The child should be able to trace letters without the help of dotted lines.

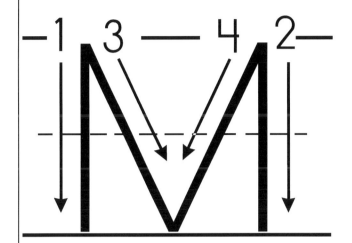

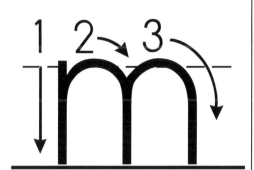

M is for **M**ouse

Have your child trace the letters "M" and "m" on the dotted line. Follow the direction and sequence shown in the example below.

Have your child trace the letters "M" and "m" on the dotted line. Follow the direction and sequence shown in the example below.

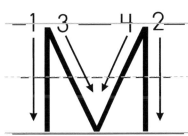

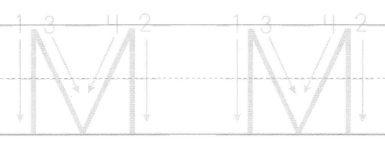

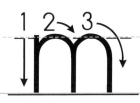

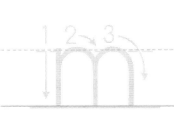

Have your child trace the letters "M" and "m" on the dotted line.

Trace and Learn Letters - Alphabet Tracing Practice Workbook

Have your child trace the letters "M" and "m" on the dotted line.

Have your child trace the letters "M" and "m" on the lines below. Follow the direction and sequence shown in the example. The child should be able to trace letters without the help of dotted lines.

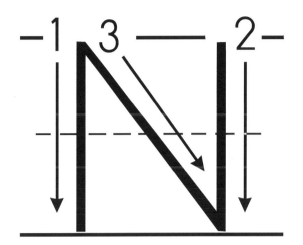 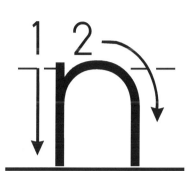

N is for **N**arwhal

Have your child trace the letters "N" and "n" on the dotted line. Follow the direction and sequence shown in the example below.

Trace and Learn Letters - Alphabet Tracing Practice Workbook

Have your child trace the letters "N" and "n" on the dotted line. Follow the direction and sequence shown in the example below.

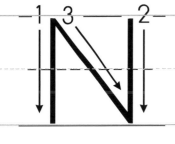

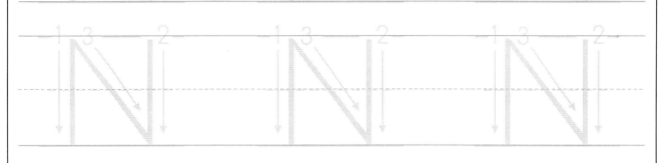
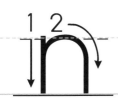

Have your child trace the letters "N" and "n" on the dotted line.

Have your child trace the letters "N" and "n" on the dotted line.

Have your child trace the letters "N" and "n" on the lines below. Follow the direction and sequence shown in the example. The child should be able to trace letters without the help of dotted lines.

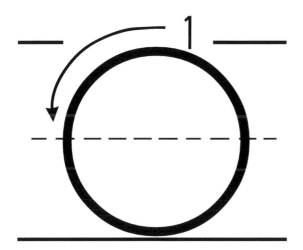

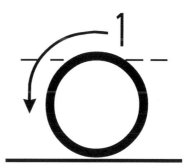

O is for Owl

Have your child trace the letters "O" and "o" on the dotted line. Follow the direction and sequence shown in the example below.

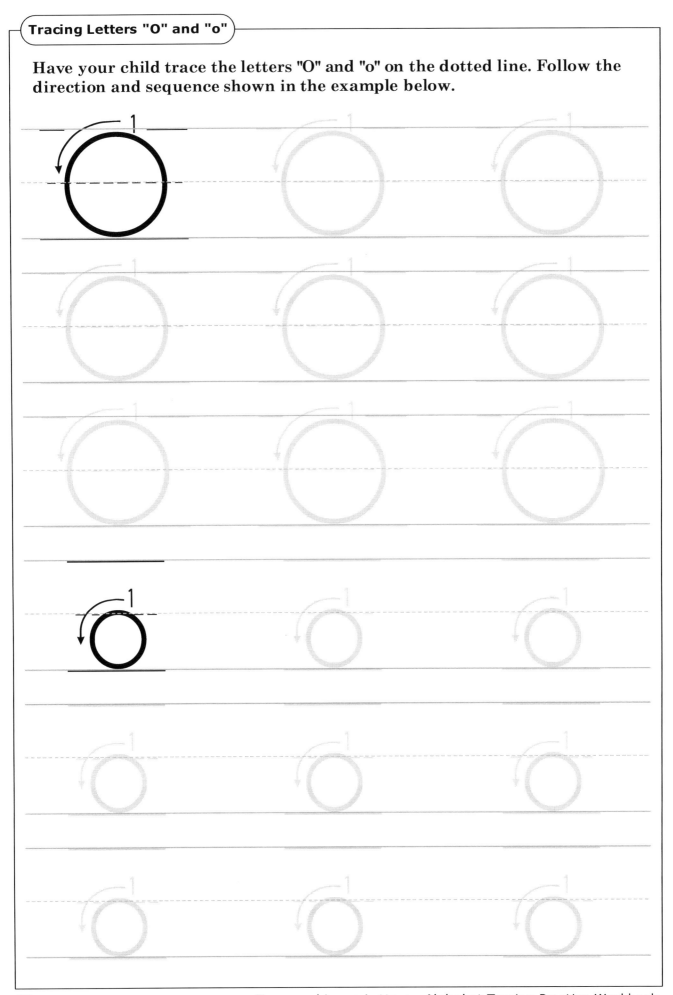

Have your child trace the letters "O" and "o" on the dotted line. Follow the direction and sequence shown in the example below.

Have your child trace the letters "O" and "o" on the dotted line.

Trace and Learn Letters - Alphabet Tracing Practice Workbook

Have your child trace the letters "O" and "o" on the dotted line.

Have your child trace the letters "O" and "o" on the lines below. Follow the direction and sequence shown in the example. The child should be able to trace letters without the help of dotted lines.

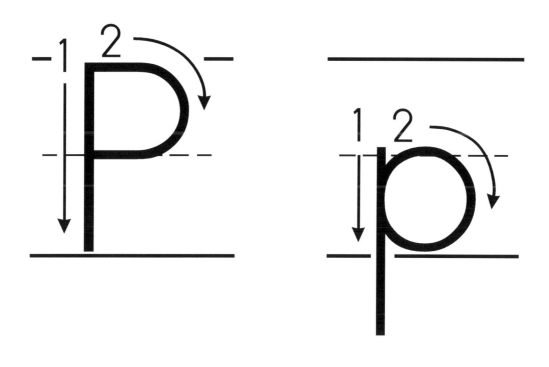

P is for **P**ig

Have your child trace the letters "P" and "p" on the dotted line. Follow the direction and sequence shown in the example below.

Trace and Learn Letters - Alphabet Tracing Practice Workbook

Have your child trace the letters "P" and "p" on the dotted line. Follow the direction and sequence shown in the example below.

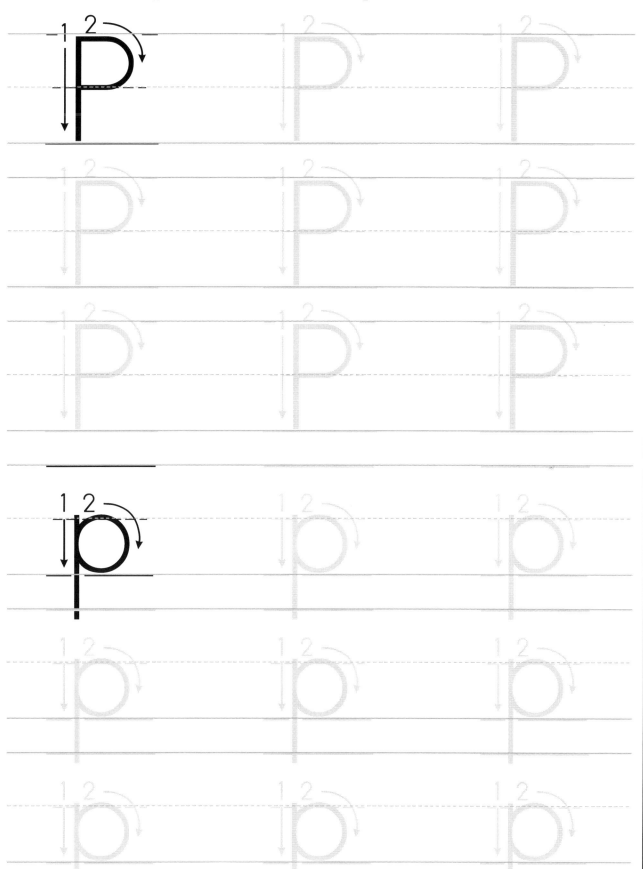

Have your child trace the letters "P" and "p" on the dotted line.

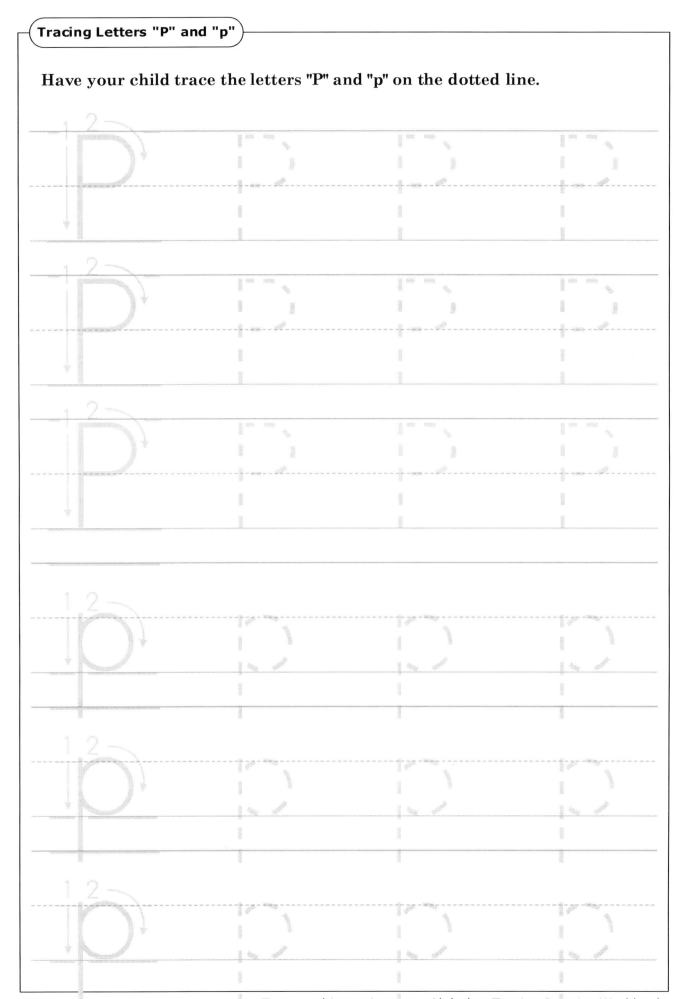

Have your child trace the letters "P" and "p" on the dotted line.

Have your child trace the letters "P" and "p" on the lines below. Follow the direction and sequence shown in the example. The child should be able to trace letters without the help of dotted lines.

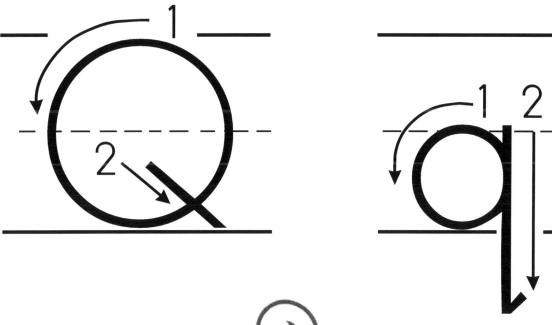

Q is for Quail

Have your child trace the letters "Q" and "q" on the dotted line. Follow the direction and sequence shown in the example below.

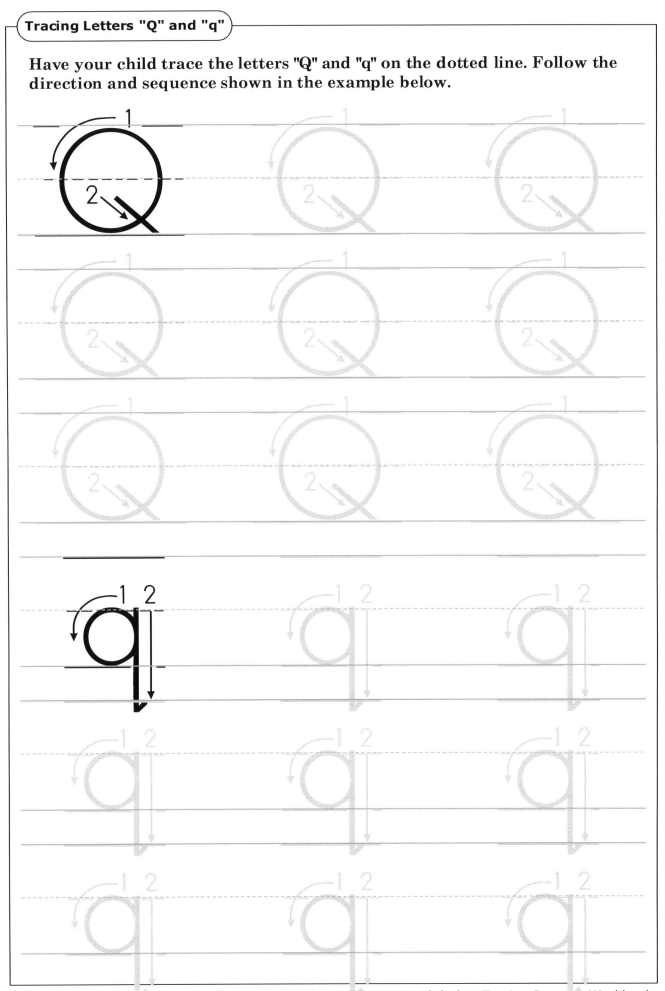

Have your child trace the letters "Q" and "q" on the dotted line. Follow the direction and sequence shown in the example below.

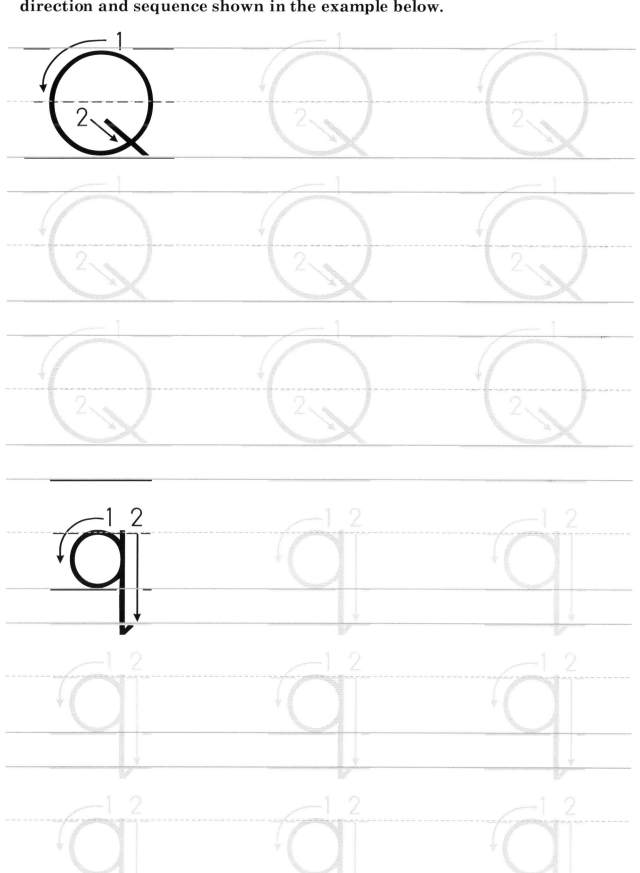

Have your child trace the letters "Q" and "q" on the dotted line.

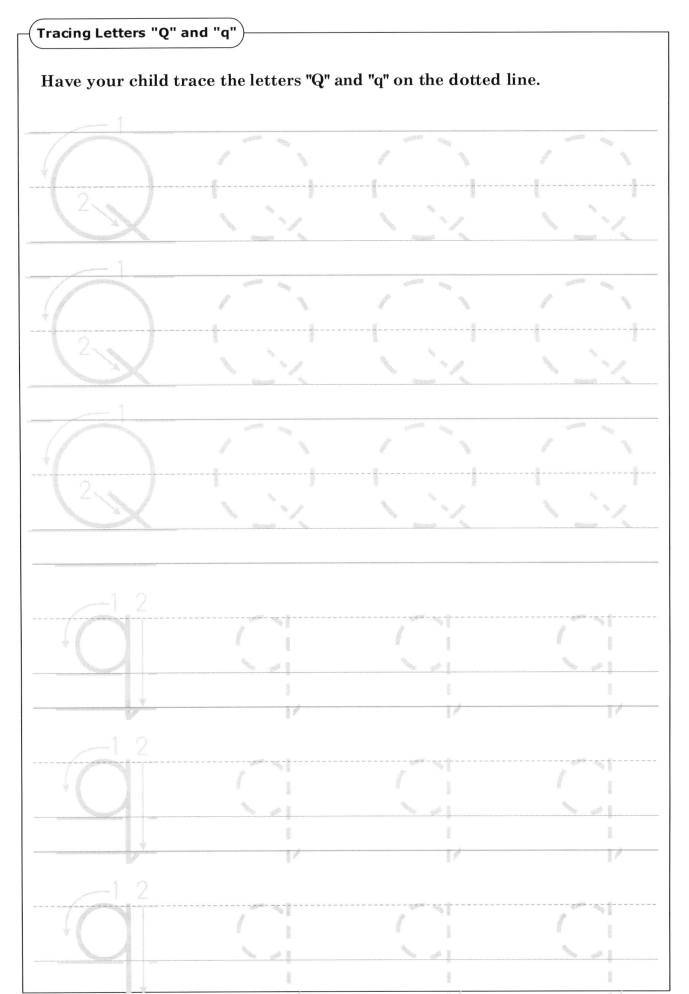

Trace and Learn Letters - Alphabet Tracing Practice Workbook

Have your child trace the letters "Q" and "q" on the dotted line.

Have your child trace the letters "Q" and "q" on the lines below. Follow the direction and sequence shown in the example. The child should be able to trace letters without the help of dotted lines.

Trace and Learn Letters - Alphabet Tracing Practice Workbook

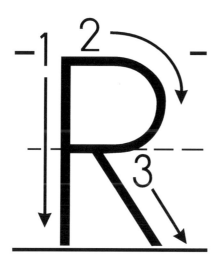
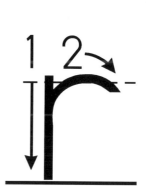

R is for **R**accoon

Have your child trace the letters "R" and "r" on the dotted line. Follow the direction and sequence shown in the example below.

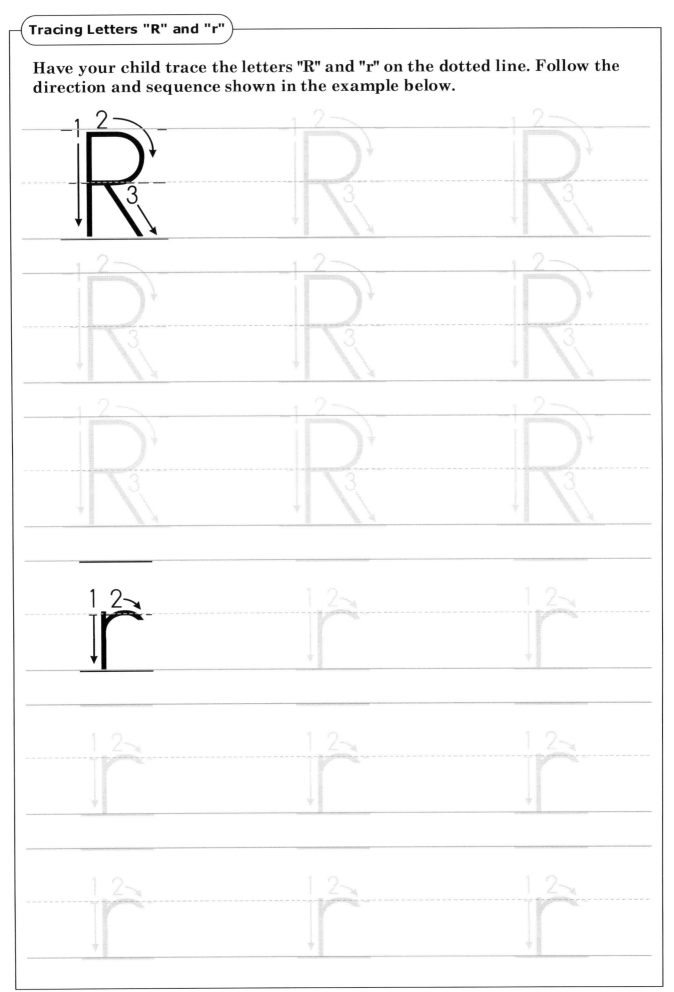

Have your child trace the letters "R" and "r" on the dotted line. Follow the direction and sequence shown in the example below.

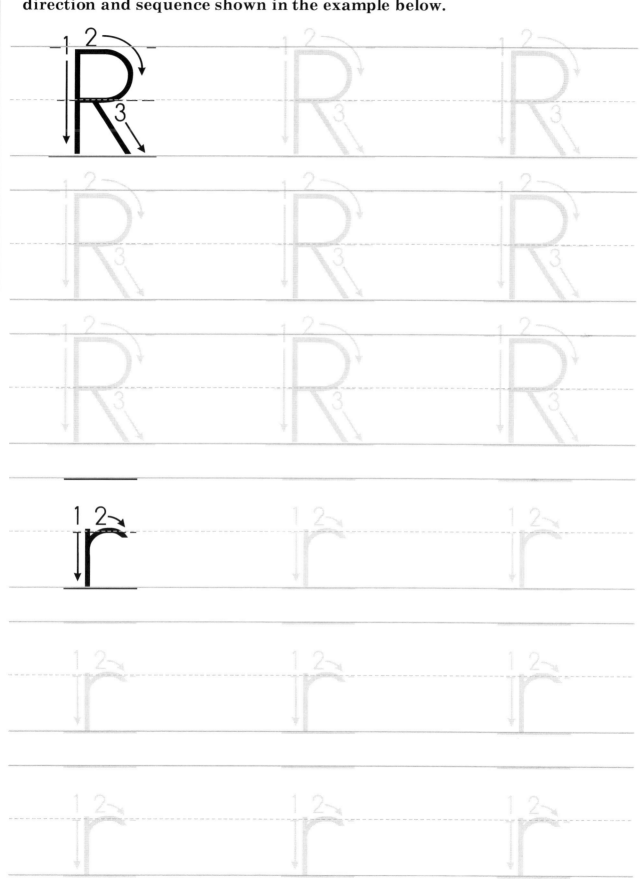

Have your child trace the letters "R" and "r" on the dotted line.

Trace and Learn Letters - Alphabet Tracing Practice Workbook

Have your child trace the letters "R" and "r" on the dotted line.

Have your child trace the letters "R" and "r" on the lines below. Follow the direction and sequence shown in the example. The child should be able to trace letters without the help of dotted lines.

Trace and Learn Letters - Alphabet Tracing Practice Workbook

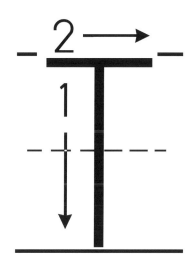
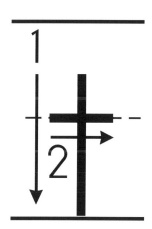

T is for **T**urtle

Have your child trace the letters "T" and "t" on the dotted line. Follow the direction and sequence shown in the example below.

Have your child trace the letters "T" and "t" on the dotted line. Follow the direction and sequence shown in the example below.

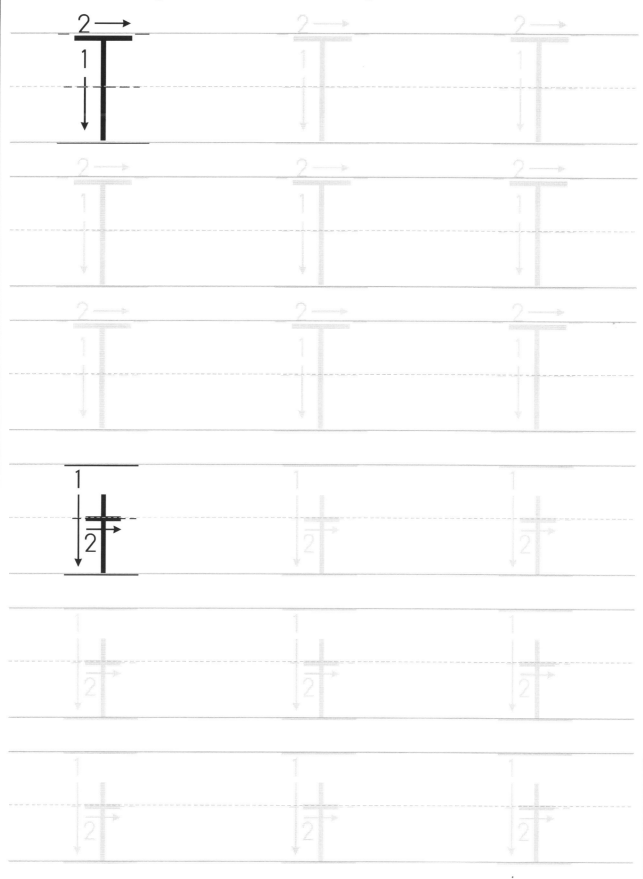

Have your child trace the letters "T" and "t" on the dotted line.

ok   Trace and Learn Letters - Alphabet Tracing Practice Workbook

Have your child trace the letters "T" and "t" on the dotted line.

Have your child trace the letters "T" and "t" on the lines below. Follow the direction and sequence shown in the example. The child should be able to trace letters without the help of dotted lines.

Trace and Learn Letters - Alphabet Tracing Practice Workbook

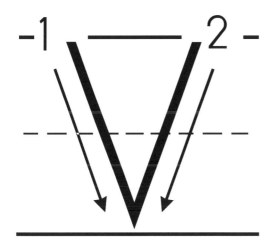
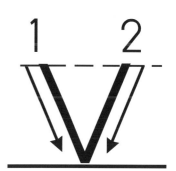

V is for **V**ulture

Have your child trace the letters "V" and "v" on the dotted line. Follow the direction and sequence shown in the example below.

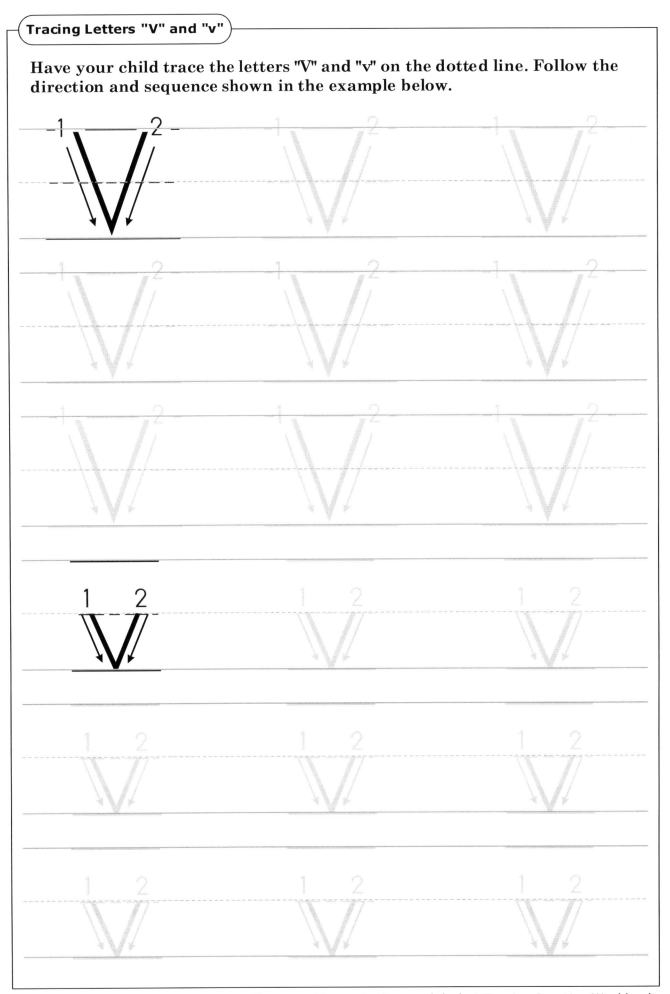

Trace and Learn Letters - Alphabet Tracing Practice Workbook

Have your child trace the letters "V" and "v" on the dotted line. Follow the direction and sequence shown in the example below.

Have your child trace the letters "V" and "v" on the dotted line.

Trace and Learn Letters - Alphabet Tracing Practice Workbook

Have your child trace the letters "V" and "v" on the dotted line.

Have your child trace the letters "V" and "v" on the lines below. Follow the direction and sequence shown in the example. The child should be able to trace letters without the help of dotted lines.

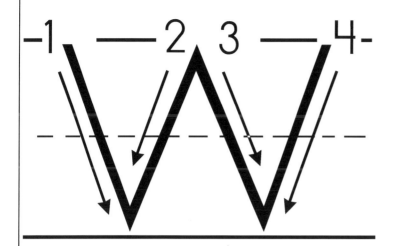

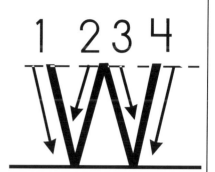

W is for **W**hale

Have your child trace the letters "W" and "w" on the dotted line. Follow the direction and sequence shown in the example below.

Have your child trace the letters "W" and "w" on the dotted line. Follow the direction and sequence shown in the example below.

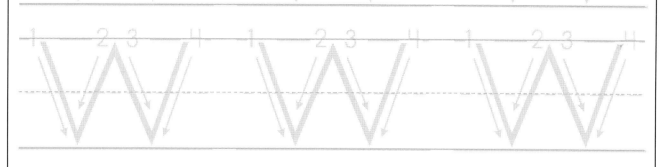

Have your child trace the letters "W" and "w" on the dotted line.

Have your child trace the letters "W" and "w" on the dotted line.

Have your child trace the letters "W" and "w" on the lines below. Follow the direction and sequence shown in the example. The child should be able to trace letters without the help of dotted lines.

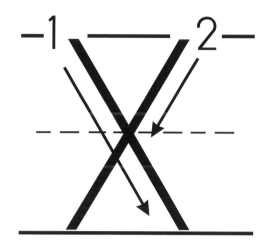 

X is for **X**-ray Fish

Have your child trace the letters "X" and "x" on the dotted line. Follow the direction and sequence shown in the example below.

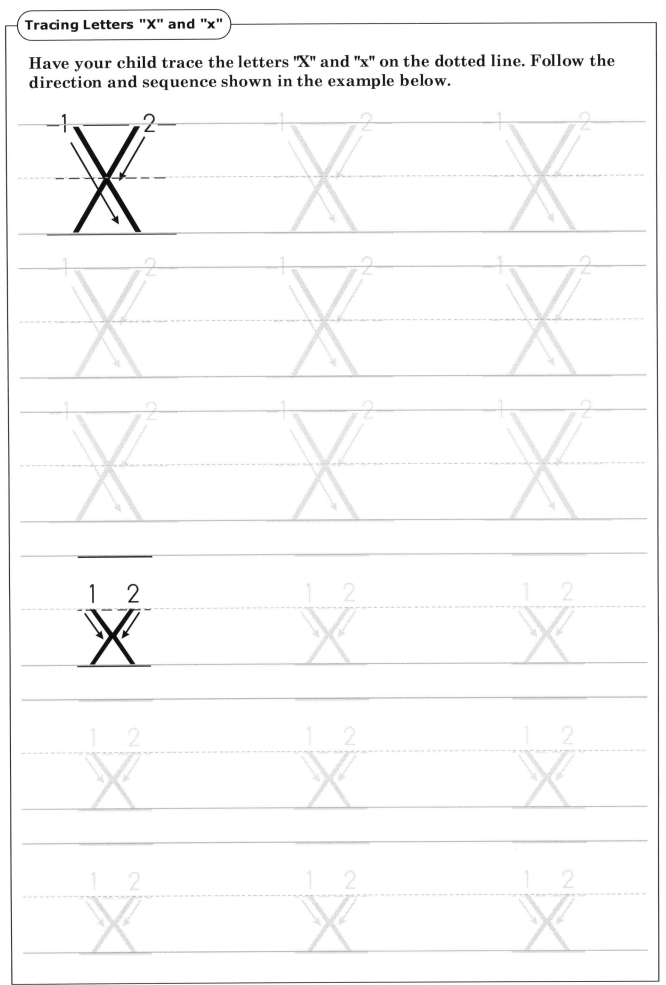

Have your child trace the letters "X" and "x" on the dotted line. Follow the direction and sequence shown in the example below.

Have your child trace the letters "X" and "x" on the dotted line.

Trace and Learn Letters - Alphabet Tracing Practice Workbook

Have your child trace the letters "X" and "x" on the dotted line.

Have your child trace the letters "X" and "x" on the lines below. Follow the direction and sequence shown in the example. The child should be able to trace letters without the help of dotted lines.

Trace and Learn Letters - Alphabet Tracing Practice Workbook

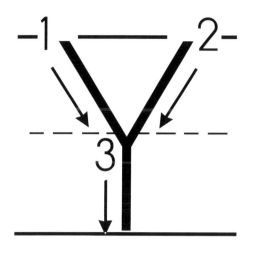

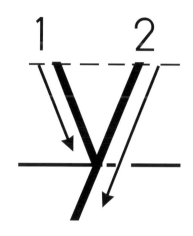

Y is for Yak

Have your child trace the letters "Y" and "y" on the dotted line. Follow the direction and sequence shown in the example below.

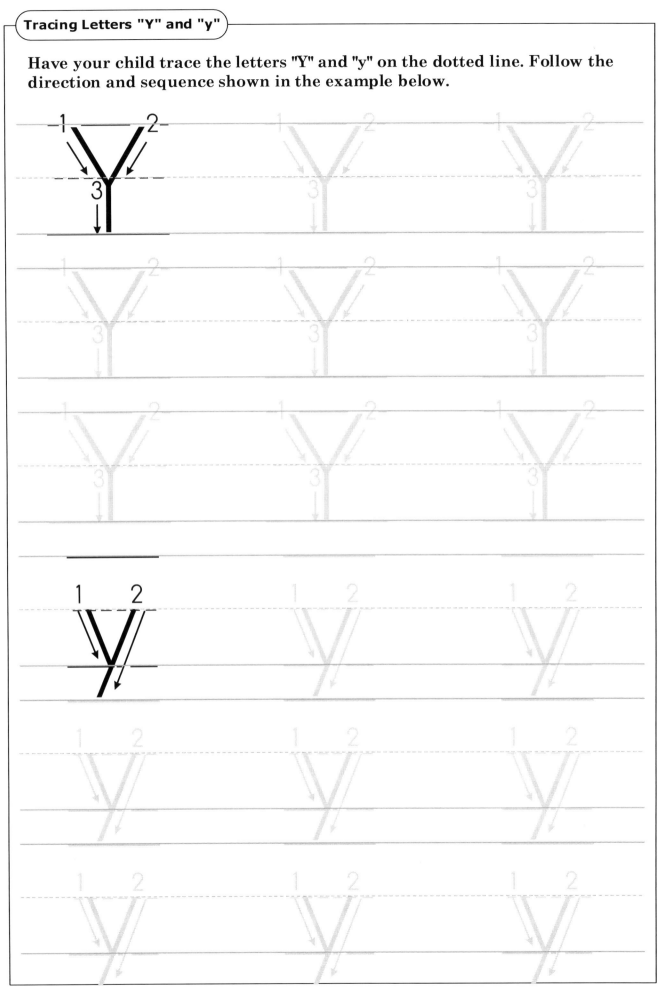

Have your child trace the letters "Y" and "y" on the dotted line. Follow the direction and sequence shown in the example below.

Have your child trace the letters "Y" and "y" on the dotted line.

Trace and Learn Letters - Alphabet Tracing Practice Workbook

Have your child trace the letters "Y" and "y" on the dotted line.

Have your child trace the letters "Y" and "y" on the lines below. Follow the direction and sequence shown in the example. The child should be able to trace letters without the help of dotted lines.

Trace and Learn Letters - Alphabet Tracing Practice Workbook

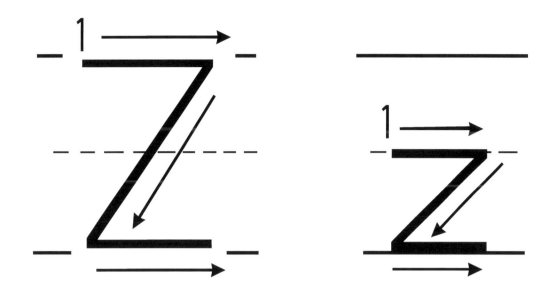

Z is for **Z**ebra

Have your child trace the letters "Z" and "z" on the dotted line. Follow the direction and sequence shown in the example below.

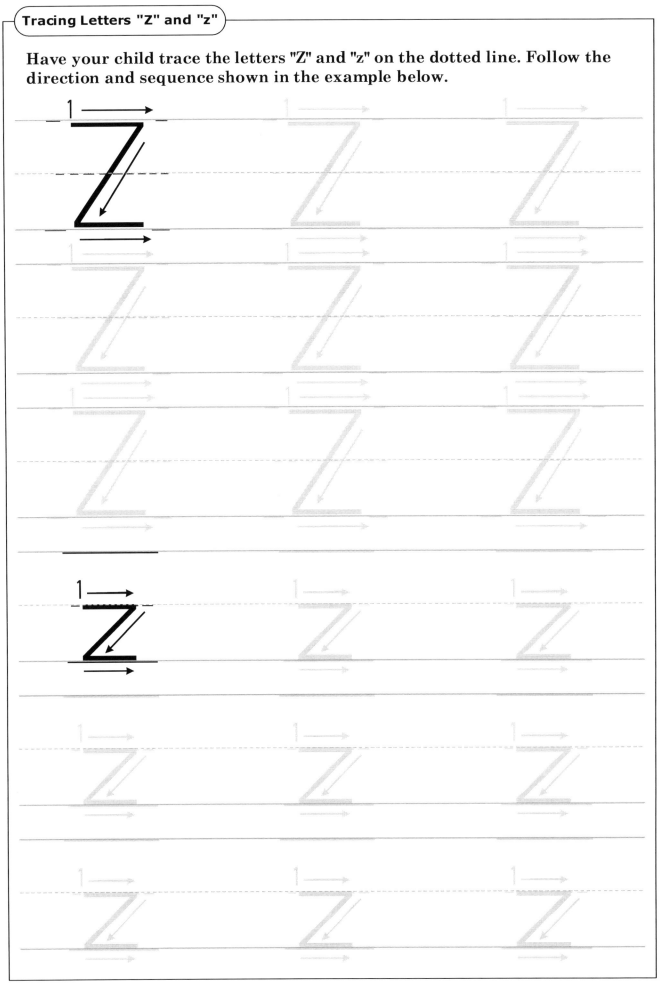

Have your child trace the letters "Z" and "z" on the dotted line. Follow the direction and sequence shown in the example below.

Have your child trace the letters "Z" and "z" on the dotted line.

Trace and Learn Letters - Alphabet Tracing Practice Workbook

Have your child trace the letters "Z" and "z" on the dotted line.

Have your child trace the letters "Z" and "z" on the lines below. Follow the direction and sequence shown in the example. The child should be able to trace letters without the help of dotted lines.

64726972R00089

Made in the USA
Lexington, KY
17 June 2017